The Road Trip

by Pamela Rushby

illustrated by Nathalie Beauvois

OXFORD
UNIVERSITY PRESS
AUSTRALIA & NEW ZEALAND

Mum, Dad, Harry and Ava went on a road trip in the car.

They saw a reef, a rainforest and a desert. Which did they like best?

reef

rainforest

desert

They went on a boat to the reef.

The sea was so blue!

I liked swimming in the sea and looking at the fish.

reef

6

The rainforest had tall trees
and long vines.

It was hot there. It rained a lot.

I liked going up in the trees. I saw lots of birds!

reef
rainforest

It was fun to play in the vines.

Ava   Harry

11

The desert was hot. It was dry, too.
It didn't rain in the desert.

Mum, Dad, Harry and Ava went into a cave. There were bats in the cave.

I liked seeing the bats fly out of the cave.

reef

rainforest

desert

Snakes wanted to eat them.
I didn't like that!

Ava	Harry
👍	👎
👍	👍
👍	👎